HOW TO MASTER ASSERTIVENESS

Conquer Self-Doubt, Boost Self-Confidence, Cultivate Positive Self-Talk, and Become the Best Version of Yourself.

PRADIP DAS

reliable, complete information. No warranties of any kind are declared or implied. Readers acknowledge that the author is not engaging in the rendering of legal, financial, medical or professional advice. The content within this book has been derived from various sources. Please consult a licensed professional before attempting any techniques outlined in this book.

By reading this document, the reader agrees that under no circumstances is the author responsible for any losses, direct or indirect, which are incurred as a result of the use of information contained within this document, including, but not limited to, — errors, omissions, or inaccuracies.

CLICK HERE

Table of Contents

Introduction

Puja was known for her warm heart and infectious laughter, but behind that cheerful exterior, Puja harbored a common struggle many of us face – the challenge of expressing herself assertively.

One day, while volunteering at the local community center, Puja found herself overwhelmed with tasks. She was graciously helping everyone but failed to voice her own needs. As a result, she ended up feeling exhausted and unappreciated. It was in this moment of reflection that Puja realized the transformative power of assertiveness.

Assertiveness is like a compass guiding us through the intricate landscapes of our personal and professional lives. It is the ability to communicate our thoughts, feelings, and needs with confidence and clarity, while also respecting the rights and boundaries of others.

Defining Assertiveness:

Ever wondered how to communicate openly without being overly aggressive or overly passive? What if you could find that sweet spot where strength meets grace, allowing you to face life's challenges with confidence? Enter assertiveness – the art of expressing yourself firmly yet gently. It's like a dance, where you navigate the delicate balance between being straightforward and maintaining a sense of kindness. Ready to unravel the secrets of assertiveness and master the art of confident communication?

In Puja's case, embracing assertiveness meant learning to communicate her limits, say 'no' when needed, and stand up for her own well-being. As she embarked on this journey, she discovered that assertiveness was not about changing who she was but rather about embracing her authentic self and valuing her own needs.

Importance of Assertiveness:

During the initial stages of my career, one of my seniors advised me to develop more assertiveness for personal and professional growth. At that time, I didn't understand the significance of this advice. However, with time, I came to recognize that assertiveness is a critical skill for increased productivity without compromising anyone's self-esteem.

Imagine a workplace where colleagues express their ideas confidently, collaborate seamlessly, and address conflicts with open communication. Picture personal relationships thriving on mutual respect, where individuals feel heard and understood. This is the impact of assertiveness.

In our personal lives, assertiveness nurtures healthy connections by fostering mutual understanding and empathy. It strengthens our ability to express love, gratitude, and concern, leading to more meaningful relationships.

Professionally, assertiveness is a key ingredient for success. It empowers individuals to negotiate effectively, advocate for their ideas, and navigate the complexities of teamwork. Employers value assertive team members for their clarity, problem-solving skills, and the positive impact they bring to the workplace culture.

As we explore deeper into the chapters ahead, let Puja's journey serve as a reminder that assertiveness is not just a skill; it's a pathway to a more authentic, fulfilling, and empowered life.

Mastering Assertiveness for a Fulfilling Life

In a world buzzing with diverse interactions and relationships, the ability to express oneself with clarity, confidence, and empathy becomes paramount. It is this realization that forms the heartbeat of our journey through "How to Master Assertiveness." This book is not just a guide; it's an invitation to embark on a transformative exploration of self-discovery, communication enhancement, and the cultivation of a more assertive and fulfilling life.

Understanding the Core Essence: This book emphasizes that assertiveness doesn't work the same way for everyone. It is a dynamic skill that evolves with each individual's unique experiences, challenges, and aspirations. Whether you find yourself in the intricate dance of personal relationships or navigating the complexities of the professional realm, mastering assertiveness becomes a compass guiding you towards authentic self-expression.

A Holistic Approach to Personal Growth: This book goes beyond mere tips and techniques. It offers a holistic approach to personal growth, emphasizing that assertiveness is not just a tool but a way of life. By researching into the psychological foundations of assertiveness, readers will gain insights into the roots of their communication styles, paving the way for lasting transformation.

Each chapter acts as a stepping stone in this journey, addressing different aspects of assertiveness. From understanding the benefits and identifying personal assertiveness styles to overcoming barriers and honing practical skills, we will follow a roadmap to enhance communication in both personal and professional aspects.

Practical Applications in Daily Life: One of the unique features of this book is its commitment to practicality. The wisdom shared within these pages is not meant to be theoretical but deeply applicable to real-life situations. Through practical examples, readers will be equipped with the tools to integrate assertiveness seamlessly into their daily interactions. Whether you are aiming to enhance your communication at work, in your relationships, or within yourself, the practical applications explored in this book will serve as a guide for immediate and sustainable change.

A Call to Ongoing Growth: Assertiveness is not a destination but a continuous process of self-reflection and refinement. The final chapters will guide readers on how to integrate assertiveness into their daily routines, foster habits that strengthen this skill, and encourage a mindset that embraces lifelong learning.

Resources for Further Learning: To empower readers beyond the pages of this book, a comprehensive appendix provides additional resources, worksheets, and exercises. These tools are crafted to support readers in their ongoing commitment to mastering assertiveness, ensuring that the lessons learned become integral to their personal and professional evolution.

"How to Master Assertiveness" is like a caring friend, not your usual self-help book. It's a guide for those who want more than just learning a skill – it's about becoming a person who values themselves, builds good relationships, and succeeds in both personal and professional life. As you read, I hope you not only get advice but also feel inspired to start your

own journey to being more confident and living a genuine, strong, and happy life.

Understanding Assertiveness

Assertiveness involves the art of expressing oneself openly and honestly while respecting the rights and boundaries of others. To truly comprehend the essence of assertiveness, it is essential to explore its nuances and distinguish it from its counterparts – aggressiveness and passivity.

Consider the scenario of a team meeting where ideas are being discussed. An assertive individual might express their thoughts clearly, listen actively to others, and collaborate openly. On the contrary, an aggressive person may dominate the conversation, dismissing opposing views, while a passive individual might withhold their input, avoiding potential conflict.

Differentiating Assertiveness from Aggressiveness and Passivity:

Understanding the fine line between assertiveness, aggressiveness, and passivity is crucial for cultivating healthy communication.

Assertive people clearly expresses thoughts, feelings, and needs. They listen actively to others' viewpoints and value one's rights while respecting others'.

Example: Saying "I feel overwhelmed with my current workload; can we discuss how to redistribute tasks?" in a team meeting.

Aggressive people dominates conversations, often disregarding others. Uses harsh language or a confrontational tone. They disregards others' feelings and rights.

Example: Interrupting a colleague and saying, "Your ideas are always irrelevant; let's focus on what actually matters."

Passive people avoids expressing thoughts or needs. They may agree with others to avoid conflict and later they feel powerless or unimportant.

Example: Agreeing to take on extra work even when overwhelmed, without expressing concerns.

Assertiveness involves finding the middle ground – expressing oneself authentically while respecting the perspectives of others.

The Psychological Foundations of Assertiveness: To grasp assertiveness at its core, it's essential to go deeper to its psychological underpinnings.

Self-Awareness: Recognizing and understanding one's emotions, thoughts, and values.

Example: Reflecting on personal boundaries and recognizing when they are being compromised.

Self-Expression: Effectively conveying one's thoughts, feelings, and needs.

Example: Communicating concerns or desires openly and honestly in a relationship or professional setting.

Self-Respect: Acknowledging one's worth and rights without infringing on others'.

Example: Politely but firmly declining additional tasks when already overwhelmed at work.

The Impact of Assertiveness on Relationships and Self-Esteem: Assertiveness is a dynamic force influencing the quality of relationships and individual self-esteem.

Positive Impact on Relationships: Fosters open communication and mutual understanding. Builds trust and respect among individuals.

Example: Resolving conflicts constructively by expressing concerns and actively listening to the other party.

Enhanced Self-Esteem: Affirms one's ability to communicate effectively and navigate social interactions. Encourages a positive self-perception.

Example: Successfully negotiating a job offer, reinforcing a sense of competence.

Conflict Resolution: Equip individuals to address conflicts without resorting to aggression or avoidance. Promotes healthier relationships through constructive dialogue.

Example: Addressing a disagreement with a friend by expressing feelings and seeking resolution.

Understanding assertiveness goes beyond surface-level communication skills; it involves a profound awareness of oneself, an ability to express authentically, and a commitment to nurturing healthy relationships and self-esteem. Mastering this delicate balance is the key to transformation in both personal and professional realms.

Benefits of Mastering Assertiveness

Assertiveness is not merely a communication skill; it is a powerful tool that can shape the course of one's personal and professional life. Mastering assertiveness opens the door to a myriad of benefits, empowering individuals to navigate the complexities of relationships, enhance self-confidence, and foster success in various aspects of life.

Improves Communication Skills

Mastering assertiveness brings about a significant enhancement in communication skills, a transformation that goes beyond words and resonates in every interaction. Let's delve into the benefits, illustrated through examples and short stories that showcase the power of assertive communication.

Enhances Clarity:

Kiran, a marketing professional, once faced a daunting challenge during a high-stakes presentation. Known for his creative ideas, Kiran often found it difficult to articulate his thoughts clearly in group settings. However, his transformative journey toward assertiveness was about to shine through.

As the meeting unfolded in the sleek conference room, discussions buzzed around a crucial campaign strategy. In the past, Kiran would feel the weight of uncertainty, struggling to convey his ideas effectively. This time, armed with the newfound power of assertiveness, he took a deep breath and raised his hand.

"I suggest we pivot our approach and tap into the untapped market segment. It aligns with our brand's image, and I believe it could lead to significant engagement," Kiran asserted with newfound confidence.

His succinct expression of ideas resonated throughout the room. The clarity in his communication not only conveyed a compelling vision but also captured the attention and respect of his colleagues. The room fell silent for a moment as everyone absorbed the impact of Kiran's assertive contribution.

As the meeting progressed, Kiran continued to navigate the discussions with precision, offering valuable insights that elevated the entire team's perspective. The transformation was palpable – from struggling to find the right words to becoming a beacon of clarity in the room.

Kiran's journey toward enhanced clarity through assertiveness not only brought recognition but also opened new doors for collaboration and leadership opportunities. The once-muted ideas now reverberated with confidence, leaving an indelible mark on the trajectory of projects and, more importantly, on Kiran's self-esteem.

Now, Kiran's assertive voice became a catalyst for innovation and collaboration. His story proves that clarity in communication not only amplifies individual impact but also inspires a collective brilliance that propels teams toward success.

Active Listening:

Our team leader, Kapil wanted us to try something new in our meetings – it's called active listening. In our important brainstorming session, he explained the idea to us. He said, "Let's really listen to each other's ideas and understand them." Rani, one of our team members, shared her idea for the marketing campaign using social media influencers. Kapil thought it was interesting and asked more about it. Then, he asked Ranjit about his thoughts on the project management system. Ranjit suggested a simpler way to work, making things more efficient. Kapil, using active listening, asked Ranjit to explain more about how it would fit with our current way of working. Ranjit explained, "It'll make tasks easier and help us work better." Kapil thanked him and said that using active listening was making our ideas come together. The whole team started to feel more excited and worked together better. Just with this small change, Kapil made our team more connected and collaborative. Now, we have a culture where everyone's ideas are heard and built upon.

Constructive Feedback:

Pratibha gathered her team for performance reviews. Addressing Avinash, she acknowledged the great initiative in his recent project but pointed out some communication gaps. Avinash, initially thinking everything was on track, appreciated Pratibha's feedback and committed to fine-tuning his communication for better team understanding. Encouraged by Avinash's response, Pratibha shifted her attention to Puja, praising her fantastic attention to detail while noting a slip in timelines on the last project. Puja acknowledged the challenge, attributing it to tight deadlines. Pratibha reassured Puja, expressing understanding, and suggested collaborating on a strategy for smoother timelines without compromising Pratibha's precision. Grateful for the constructive feedback, Pratibha pledged to brainstorm solutions. In this simple and effective exchange, Pratibha's assertive communication fostered an atmosphere of collaboration and continuous improvement within the team.

Empathetic Expression:

In the office, Ram is known for being good at both speaking up and understanding others. One day, he saw a colleague having a hard time with a tough project. Instead of just pointing out the problems, Ram took a different approach. He showed real empathy and said, "I know this project is tough. Let's figure out how we can solve it together."

Ram's way of leading shows that he's good at dealing with problems while also caring about others. By showing he understands and offering help, Ram not only made his colleague feel more confident but also made the team feel like they can work together through challenges. This caring way of leading helped the team feel close-knit, knowing they can support each other through tough times.

Effective Negotiation:

Nitin showed how to communicate assertively during negotiations for high value deal. He was dealing with a complicated deal but didn't choose to be too passive or too aggressive. Instead, Nitin used assertiveness by clearly stating what he needed. He said, "I like your proposal, but I think we can find a fair solution for both of us." This smart and friendly way didn't just help Nitin get what he wanted, but it also set up good relationships for the future. Nitin proved that being clear and working together can lead to successful business partnerships by creating an atmosphere of respect and compromise.

Resolve Misunderstandings:

In his personal relationship, Alex showed he knew how to use assertiveness to fix misunderstandings.

Instead of keeping problems to himself, he talked about them when they came up. Alex used "I" statements to share his feelings, making it a safe space for open conversation. This not only helped him express himself but also encouraged his partner to share their thoughts. It made their relationship stronger by creating understanding. Alex's use of assertiveness shows that clear communication is a powerful tool for dealing with misunderstandings, building a connection based on empathy, understanding, and respect.

In these examples, the benefits of improved communication skills through assertiveness become evident. Clarity, active listening, constructive feedback, empathetic expression, effective negotiation, and conflict resolution are not just communication tools; they are the building blocks of meaningful connections and successful interactions. As individuals embrace assertiveness, they discover the profound impact of clear and empathetic communication on their personal and professional relationships.

Enhanced Self-Confidence

Mastering assertiveness is a transformative journey that significantly enhances self-confidence, influencing various facets of an individual's personal and professional life.

Self-Affirmation and Boundary Setting: Assertiveness serves as a powerful tool for self-affirmation, enabling individuals to clearly express their needs and set boundaries. By effectively communicating limits and expectations, individuals affirm their self-worth, fostering a positive self-image.

Showcasing Competence and Accomplishments: The ability to assertively present ideas and insights is pivotal in showcasing competence and accomplishments. Assertive communication not only boosts confidence but also allows individuals to actively contribute in diverse work settings, establishing their value within a team or organization.

Promoting Personal Growth and Stepping Out of Comfort Zones: Assertiveness plays a crucial role in personal growth by encouraging individuals to step out of their comfort zones. By embracing assertiveness, individuals venture into new territories, broadening their horizons and creating opportunities for continuous development and learning.

Ownership of Choices and Actions: A fundamental aspect of assertiveness is the ownership of choices and actions. Assertive communication empowers individuals to take charge of their decisions, aligning their professional and personal journeys with their goals. This sense of ownership instills profound confidence in shaping one's destiny.

Autonomy in Decision-Making and Leadership: In decision-making and leadership roles, assertiveness establishes autonomy and confidence. The ability to assertively communicate decisions while considering input from others creates a positive and collaborative environment. Assertive leadership fosters confidence among team members and contributes to successful outcomes.

Building Resilience through Assertive Coping: Assertiveness plays a crucial role in building resilience by enabling effective coping with challenges and feedback. Rather than internalizing criticism, assertive individuals seek clarification and express their perspectives constructively. This resilient approach not only improves professional performance but fortifies self-confidence in navigating complex and challenging situations.

In short, mastering assertiveness is a means to cultivate self-confidence across diverse aspects of life. From setting boundaries to showcasing competence, promoting personal growth, and building resilience, assertiveness empowers individuals to navigate life's complexities with confidence and authenticity.

Building Healthy Relationships

Building healthy relationships is an art that demands a delicate balance of communication, empathy, and mutual respect. Assertiveness, serving as a guiding force, plays a pivotal role in crafting connections that are robust and authentic. Let's explore the intricate ways in which assertiveness contributes to the fabric of healthy relationships.

Fostering Mutual Respect: Assertiveness contributes to fostering mutual respect in relationships. Jane, an assertive colleague, noticed her ideas consistently overlooked in team meetings. By assertively sharing her thoughts, emphasizing the importance of diverse perspectives, the team dynamic shifted, fostering mutual respect and recognition for each member's contributions.

Establishing Clear Boundaries: Assertive communication is key to establishing clear boundaries in relationships. Sarah, known for her accommodating nature, set clear boundaries through assertive communication, expressing her availability and limitations. This resulted in a more balanced workload and deeper, more respectful relationships that valued Sarah's well-being.

Conflict Resolution: Assertiveness plays a crucial role in resolving conflicts within relationships. Alex and Rachel, close friends, faced a rift when Rachel felt her opinions were consistently dismissed. Alex chose to address the issue assertively, openly expressing his willingness to listen and understand. Navigating the conflict together strengthened their friendship through respectful communication.

Expressing Vulnerability: Assertive vulnerability is a powerful tool in relationships. Tom, typically reserved about his emotions, learned the power of assertive vulnerability by sharing his feelings assertively with his partner. This deepened their emotional connection and created a safe space for reciprocal sharing.

Encouraging Open Communication: Assertiveness fosters a culture of open communication in relationships. Emily, a team leader, encouraged assertive expression of ideas, concerns, and feedback among team members, creating an environment where everyone felt heard. This improved productivity and forged a sense of unity among team members.

Negotiating and Compromising: Assertiveness is instrumental in negotiating and compromising in relationships. Mike and Lily, a couple facing a major life decision, used assertiveness to openly express their preferences, concerns, and priorities. This led to a compromise that honored both their individual needs and the shared goals of their relationship.

Acknowledging Individual Differences: Assertiveness helps navigate individual differences in relationships. Carlos and Maria, friends with diverse interests, embraced assertiveness to openly communicate their preferences and find common ground. This approach built a relationship that celebrated individuality, fostering a bond enriched by their unique qualities.

Cultivating Emotional Intimacy: Assertiveness is vital in cultivating emotional intimacy in relationships. David and Sophia, a couple navigating the complexities of emotional intimacy, used assertiveness to express their feelings openly. Through vulnerable conversations, they deepened their connection, creating a relationship grounded in emotional understanding and support.

Assertiveness, woven into the fabric of these examples and stories, emerges as the golden thread strengthening the tapestry of healthy relationships. It empowers individuals to express themselves authentically, resolve conflicts constructively, and cultivate connections grounded in respect, empathy, and understanding. Through the lens of assertiveness, healthy relationships become not just a destination but a continual journey of growth and connection.

Professional Advancement

In the ever-evolving professional landscape, mastering assertiveness becomes a pivotal catalyst not just for survival but for thriving and advancing. This strategic communication style proves instrumental in various facets of professional growth, propelling individuals toward success and recognition.

Effective Negotiation: Assertiveness shines brightly in negotiation scenarios, as illustrated by Sarah's successful salary negotiation. Armed with market research and a clear understanding of her value, she confidently presented her case, securing not only a favorable salary but also respect for her negotiation skills, setting the stage for future advancements.

Leadership Qualities: Assertive leadership, exemplified by Alex, a mid-level manager, emerges as a powerful asset during challenging projects. Addressing conflicts openly and encouraging team members to express concerns, Alex's assertive approach not only resolved project challenges but also earned him the trust of his team, paving the way for his ascent within the organization.

Career Success: Emma, an ambitious sales professional, illustrates the significance of assertiveness in career success. Recognizing a high-stakes client meeting, she assertively pitched her ideas, emphasizing the unique value her solutions brought. This assertive move not only secured the deal but positioned Emma as a key player in future strategic discussions.

Navigating Professional Challenges: James, an IT specialist, showcases assertive problem-solving skills when faced with a technical challenge that could have derailed a critical project. Assertively communicating the issue and proposing a collaborative solution, James not only salvaged the project but demonstrated his ability to navigate challenges with confidence and professionalism.

Building a Positive Professional Image: Maya, a young professional, emphasizes the importance of assertive networking. During a conference, she assertively approached senior professionals, expressing genuine interest and seeking advice. This networking strategy expanded her professional circle, leading to mentorship opportunities and exposure to new career avenues.

Assertive Communication in Team Dynamics: Chris, a project manager, leverages assertive communication to address internal conflicts within his team. Encouraging open dialogue and assertively addressing concerns, Chris transforms team dynamics, improving overall collaboration and elevating his reputation as a leader capable of managing and fostering a positive team environment.

Strategic Decision-Making: Ryan, a senior executive, showcases assertive decision-making in a scenario with potential organizational impact. Gathering input, considering diverse perspectives, and confidently making a decision aligned with the company's goals, Ryan's assertive approach positions him as a strategic influencer contributing to the company's success.

Assertiveness in the professional realm is not merely a communication style; it's a strategic tool for advancement. These examples and short stories illustrate that individuals who master assertiveness not only navigate professional challenges effectively but also contribute significantly to their organizations, earning the respect and trust of colleagues and superiors alike.

Identifying Your Assertiveness Style

Understanding your assertiveness style becomes a crucial step towards fostering healthy relationships and navigating life's challenges with confidence. Assertiveness, a delicate balance between passivity and aggression, is a skill that, when honed, empowers individuals to express themselves authentically.

1. Self-Reflection: Unveiling Your Natural Style

Begin by delving into introspection. Reflect on past interactions and responses to various situations. Recognize patterns in your communication – moments when you felt unheard, instances where you might have hesitated to voice your thoughts, and times when your expression might have come across as overly forceful.

2. Communication Analysis: Decode Your Verbal and Non-Verbal Cues

Examine how you convey your thoughts verbally and non-verbally. Assess your tone, pace, and the language you use. Analyze your body language – are you maintaining eye contact, employing open gestures, or displaying signs of discomfort? Understanding the nuances of your communication style unveils valuable insights into your assertiveness tendencies.

3. Assertiveness Assessment Tools: Seeking Objective Insight

Consider utilizing assertiveness assessment tools. These tools provide structured evaluations of your communication style, offering objective insights into your assertiveness levels. From self-assessment questionnaires to professional tools, these resources can be instrumental in identifying specific areas for development.

4. Feedback from Trusted Allies: External Perspectives

Seek feedback from trusted friends, family, or colleagues. External perspectives can offer a well-rounded view of your assertiveness style. Honest insights from those who know you well can pinpoint blind spots and provide valuable guidance on areas for improvement.

5. Real-Life Scenarios: Applying Assertiveness in Action

Apply your understanding of assertiveness in real-life scenarios. Practice expressing your needs, setting boundaries, and providing constructive feedback. Observe how your newfound awareness influences your interactions and the responses you receive.

6. Continuous Learning: Embracing Growth

Identifying your assertiveness style is not a one-time process but an ongoing journey. Embrace opportunities for continuous learning and refinement. As life presents new challenges, adapt your assertiveness style to align with your evolving self.

By unravelling the layers of your assertiveness style, you equip yourself with a powerful tool for effective communication, personal empowerment, and the building of meaningful connections. In the chapters to come, we'll delve deeper into strategies for enhancing and fine-tuning your assertiveness skills.

Recognizing Patterns of Behavior

Assertiveness is a nuanced aspect of communication, and understanding your assertiveness style is a crucial step toward cultivating healthier interactions and relationships. By recognizing patterns of behavior, you can gain insights into how you typically express yourself and navigate various situations. Let's explore the journey of identifying your assertiveness style.

1) The Assertive Communicator:

Patterns of Behavior:

- Expresses thoughts, feelings, and needs openly and honestly.

- Listens actively to others and values their perspectives.

- Sets clear boundaries and respects the rights of others.

Identifying Traits:

- Open communication without dominating.

- Confident expression of needs and preferences.

- Comfortable with both giving and receiving feedback.

The Aggressive Communicator:

Patterns of Behavior:

- Dominates conversations, often interrupting others.

- Uses a confrontational tone or harsh language.

- Disregards the feelings and rights of others.

Identifying Traits:

- Tends to control conversations.

- May be perceived as intimidating or disrespectful.

- Struggles with receiving feedback without defensiveness.

The Passive Communicator:

Patterns of Behavior:

- Avoids expressing thoughts, feelings, or needs.

- May agree with others to avoid conflict.

- Feels powerless or unimportant in interactions.

Identifying Traits:

- Difficulty saying 'no.'

- Tendency to downplay personal needs.

- Limited expression of personal opinions.

The Passive-Aggressive Communicator:

Patterns of Behavior:

- Indirect expression of thoughts or needs.

- Engages in subtle forms of resistance or avoidance.

- Expresses negativity covertly.

Identifying Traits:

- Reluctant agreement followed by non-compliance.

- Sarcasm or subtle undermining behavior.

- Difficulty addressing conflicts directly.

The Manipulative Communicator:

Patterns of Behavior:

- Seeks to control situations through covert means.

- Uses charm or manipulation to influence others.

- Prioritizes personal agenda over mutual respect.

Identifying Traits:

- Skilled in persuasion and influence.

- May use guilt or flattery to achieve objectives.

- Often leaves others feeling manipulated.

The Passive-Assertive Communicator:

Patterns of Behavior:

- Initially avoids conflict but expresses needs assertively when necessary.

- Balances assertiveness with a desire to maintain harmony.

- Seeks compromise without sacrificing personal rights.

Identifying Traits:

- Chooses battles selectively.

- Values open communication but avoids unnecessary conflict.

- Adapts assertiveness based on the situation.

Steps to Identify Your Assertiveness Style:

Self-Reflection:

- Consider past interactions and your typical responses to challenges.

- Reflect on situations where you felt either empowered or disempowered.

Feedback from Others:

- Seek input from trusted friends, colleagues, or mentors.

- Inquire about how your communication style is perceived in various contexts.

Journaling:

- Keep a communication journal to track your responses in different situations.

- Note instances where you felt either assertive or struggled with expression.

Professional Assessments:

- Explore personality and communication style assessments.

- Utilize tools that provide insights into assertiveness tendencies.

Identifying your assertiveness style is a continuous process of self-discovery. By recognizing your patterns of behavior, you gain the foundation to enhance your assertiveness, fostering healthier and more effective communication in all aspects of your life.

Exploring Situational Assertiveness

Situational assertiveness is the art of adapting one's assertiveness style based on the context, relationships, and specific challenges presented. Let's delve into the intricacies of exploring situational assertiveness:

Workplace Dynamics:

Scenario: Team Collaboration

In a collaborative team environment, an assertive approach might involve openly sharing ideas, actively participating in discussions, and diplomatically challenging viewpoints when necessary. Recognizing when to assert oneself, when to compromise, and when to yield fosters effective teamwork.

Personal Relationships:

Scenario: Setting Boundaries

In personal relationships, assertiveness manifests in setting and communicating boundaries. For instance, an individual might assertively express the need for personal space or communicate expectations regarding shared responsibilities. Navigating these conversations with empathy ensures that assertiveness contributes to healthy relationships.

Handling Conflict:

Scenario: Resolving Disagreements

Assertiveness plays a crucial role in conflict resolution. In situations of disagreement, an assertive individual would express their perspective while actively listening to others. This balance ensures a constructive exchange of ideas, leading to resolutions that consider diverse viewpoints.

Professional Advancement:

Scenario: Job Interview

During a job interview, an assertive approach involves confidently articulating one's achievements, skills, and career aspirations. Balancing self-assurance with humility, an assertive interviewee can make a lasting impression, showcasing qualities that align with professional advancement.

Social Settings:

Scenario: Social Gatherings

In social settings, situational assertiveness might involve initiating conversations, expressing opinions, and actively engaging with others. Recognizing the social context allows individuals to adapt their assertiveness style, ensuring they contribute positively to the social dynamic.

Authority and Subordination:

Scenario: Team Leadership

In a leadership role, an assertive leader confidently communicates expectations, provides feedback, and makes decisions. However, in situations where one is in a subordinate position, assertiveness may involve expressing concerns or suggestions respectfully, contributing to a collaborative work environment.

Crisis Management:

Scenario: Handling Crisis

During times of crisis, assertiveness takes on a strategic role. Effectively communicating plans, addressing concerns transparently, and providing reassurance when necessary are assertive actions that instill confidence and guide a team through challenging situations.

Adapting Assertiveness Styles: Recognizing the fluidity of assertiveness styles enables individuals to adapt to the demands of various situations. Being overly assertive in a delicate conversation or excessively passive in a decision-making scenario can hinder effective communication. A nuanced understanding of situational assertiveness empowers individuals to:

Assess Context:

Recognize the specific demands and nuances of each situation.

Consider the relationships involved and the potential impact of communication choices.

Flexibility:

Adapt assertiveness styles based on the dynamic nature of interpersonal interactions.

Acknowledge that what works in one context may need adjustment in another.

Strategic Communication:

Employ assertiveness strategically to achieve desired outcomes.

Utilize a balanced approach that considers the needs and perspectives of all parties involved.

Exploring situational assertiveness is a continuous journey of self-awareness and adaptability. By honing this skill, individuals can navigate the diverse landscape of communication with finesse, ensuring that their assertiveness is a valuable tool in every interpersonal scenario.

Overcoming Barriers to Assertiveness

Assertiveness, while a powerful skill, can be hindered by various barriers that individuals may face. Recognizing and overcoming these barriers is pivotal for fostering authentic communication and embracing the benefits of assertiveness. Let's delve into the common obstacles and effective strategies to break through these barriers:

Common Barriers to Assertiveness:

Assertiveness, a skill central to effective communication, can encounter various barriers that impede individuals from expressing themselves authentically. Let's explore these common obstacles in depth, accompanied by real-life examples:

Fear of Rejection:

Barrier: The apprehension that asserting oneself may lead to rejection or disapproval.

Example: Jane hesitated to voice her disagreement during team meetings, fearing that her colleagues might reject her ideas. As a result, she missed opportunities to contribute valuable insights.

Conflict Avoidance:

Barrier: A tendency to sidestep conflicts by suppressing personal opinions or needs.

Example: Mark, unwilling to confront a team member who consistently missed deadlines, chose to ignore the issue to avoid potential conflict. This avoidance strategy hindered effective problem-solving within the team.

Low Self-Esteem:

Barrier: Feeling unworthy or questioning the right to express opinions or set boundaries.

Example: Lisa, struggling with low self-esteem, refrained from proposing her ideas during brainstorming sessions, doubting their value and fearing judgment from her peers.

People-Pleasing Tendencies:

Barrier: Prioritizing others' needs over one's own to gain approval or avoid conflict.

Example: Sam consistently accepted additional workload from colleagues, even when overwhelmed, in an attempt to please others. This habit led to burnout and hindered Sam's overall well-being.

Lack of Communication Skills:

Barrier: Difficulty in expressing thoughts and needs clearly.

Example: Mike, lacking effective communication skills, struggled to articulate his concerns during team discussions, often leaving his colleagues confused about his perspectives.

Cultural or Gender Norms:

Barrier: Societal expectations dictating how individuals, based on their gender or cultural background, should communicate.

Example: Maria, influenced by traditional gender norms, hesitated to assert herself in a male-dominated workplace, fearing it might be perceived as inappropriate.

Perceived Power Imbalance:

Barrier: Feeling intimidated by individuals in positions of authority.

Example: David, an entry-level employee, refrained from sharing his innovative ideas with higher-ups, assuming they might dismiss his input due to their positions.

Unhealthy Past Experiences:

Barrier: Lingering effects of past situations where assertiveness led to negative consequences.

Example: Sarah, having experienced ridicule for expressing her opinions in a previous job, carried the fear of similar outcomes into her current workplace, inhibiting her assertiveness.

Fear of Hurting Others:

Barrier: Hesitation to assert oneself due to the fear of causing discomfort or pain to others.

Example: Nuan, reluctant to decline additional tasks from his supervisor, feared it might strain their relationship. Consequently, he often overcommitted, leading to stress and dissatisfaction.

Understanding these barriers is the first step towards overcoming them. Realizing that assertiveness is a valuable skill, not a threat, empowers individuals to navigate these challenges and embrace authentic communication for personal and professional growth.

Strategies to Overcome Fear and Anxiety in Assertiveness

Fear and anxiety often stand as formidable barriers to assertiveness, hindering individuals from expressing themselves authentically. Recognizing and addressing these emotions is crucial for unlocking the full potential of assertiveness. Here are effective strategies to overcome fear and anxiety in the context of assertiveness:

1. Identify and Understand Specific Fears:

Strategy: Begin by pinpointing the specific fears causing anxiety. Whether it's fear of rejection, conflict, or judgment, understanding the root cause is the first step towards overcoming it.

2. Challenge Negative Thoughts:

Strategy: Actively challenge negative thoughts that contribute to fear and anxiety. Replace self-doubt with positive affirmations and realistic self-appraisal. Remind yourself of past successes and instances where assertiveness had positive outcomes.

3. Visualize Positive Outcomes:

Strategy: Practice visualization techniques where you imagine assertive scenarios with positive outcomes. Visualization can help reprogram your mind to associate assertiveness with success rather than failure.

4. Gradual Exposure:

Strategy: Gradually expose yourself to assertive situations, starting with less intimidating scenarios. As you build confidence in expressing yourself, progressively tackle more challenging situations.

5. Set Realistic Goals:

Strategy: Establish small, realistic assertiveness goals. Celebrate each achievement, no matter how minor, to reinforce a sense of accomplishment and build confidence over time.

6. Deep Breathing and Relaxation Techniques:

Strategy: Practice deep breathing and relaxation exercises to manage anxiety in the moment. Deep breaths can help calm the nervous system and provide a sense of control during assertive interactions.

7. Positive Visualization:

Strategy: Use positive visualization not only for outcomes but also for the assertive process. Imagine yourself confidently expressing your thoughts and needs in a calm and composed manner.

8. Cognitive Restructuring:

Strategy: Identify and reframe irrational thoughts contributing to fear and anxiety. Instead of thinking, "I must be perfect," shift to "I am allowed to express myself imperfectly, and that's okay."

9. Seek Support:

Strategy: Share your fears and anxieties with a trusted friend, mentor, or therapist. Having a support system can provide encouragement, constructive feedback, and a perspective that helps alleviate anxiety.

10. Positive Self-Talk: - Strategy: Cultivate positive self-talk by challenging negative self-assessments. Replace self-critical thoughts with supportive and empowering affirmations.

11. Mindfulness and Present Moment Awareness: - Strategy: Practice mindfulness to stay present in the moment. Focus on the current interaction rather than anticipating future outcomes, reducing anticipatory anxiety.

12. Assertiveness Training: - Strategy: Enrol in assertiveness training programs or workshops. These structured environments offer guidance, role-playing opportunities, and practical exercises to build assertiveness skills and confidence.

13. Learn from Experience: - Strategy: Embrace assertive experiences, whether positive or

challenging, as learning opportunities. Reflect on each encounter to identify areas of improvement and acknowledge personal growth.

14. Celebrate Small Wins: - Strategy: Acknowledge and celebrate small victories in assertiveness. Recognizing progress, no matter how incremental, reinforces the positive aspects of expressing oneself assertively.

15. Focus on the Message, Not Perfection: - Strategy: Shift the focus from delivering a perfect message to effectively conveying your thoughts. Embrace the idea that assertiveness is about expressing yourself authentically, not flawlessly.

By incorporating these strategies into daily life, individuals can gradually overcome fear and anxiety associated with assertiveness. Building confidence in expressing oneself authentically is a transformative process that empowers individuals to navigate professional and personal interactions with resilience and authenticity.

Addressing Negative Thought Patterns

Negative thought patterns can act as significant barriers to assertiveness, impacting one's confidence and ability to express themselves authentically. By recognizing and addressing these patterns, individuals can cultivate a positive mindset that empowers assertiveness. Let's explore effective strategies for overcoming negative thought patterns:

Common Negative Thought Patterns:

Self-Doubt:

Pattern: Persistent questioning of one's abilities, worth, or the validity of personal opinions.

Impact: Undermines self-confidence, leading to hesitancy in expressing thoughts and needs.

Strategy: Challenge negative self-talk by acknowledging achievements, focusing on strengths, and reframing doubts into positive affirmations.

Catastrophizing:

Pattern: Imagining the worst-case scenarios or outcomes in social situations.

Impact: Creates anxiety and fear, hindering assertive communication due to anticipation of negative consequences.

Strategy: Practice mindfulness to stay present in the moment, challenge catastrophic thoughts by considering realistic outcomes, and visualize positive interactions.

Mind Reading:

Pattern: Assuming what others think or feel without concrete evidence.

Impact: Results in self-consciousness and fear of judgment, limiting assertive expression.

Strategy: Challenge assumptions by seeking clarification in communication, recognizing that one's interpretation may not align with others' perspectives.

Perfectionism:

Pattern: Setting unrealistically high standards for oneself, fearing failure or criticism.

Impact: Hinders assertiveness by fostering a fear of not meeting perceived expectations.

Strategy: Embrace imperfection as a part of the learning process. Set realistic goals, celebrate progress, and acknowledge that mistakes contribute to growth.

Filtering:

Pattern: Focusing solely on negative aspects of a situation while dismissing positive aspects.

Impact: Diminishes self-esteem and amplifies fear of negative outcomes.

Strategy: Challenge negative filtering by consciously recognizing positive aspects of situations and interactions. Cultivate a balanced perspective.

Labeling:

Pattern: Applying negative labels or judgments to oneself based on past experiences.

Impact: Reinforces a negative self-image, limiting the belief in one's right to assertiveness.

Strategy: Replace self-labeling with positive affirmations. Focus on personal growth and acknowledge the capacity for change.

Overgeneralization:

Pattern: Drawing broad conclusions about oneself based on isolated incidents.

Impact: Creates a sense of hopelessness and discouragement, hindering assertive behavior.

Strategy: Challenge overgeneralization by recognizing that isolated incidents do not define overall competence or worth. Consider individual situations independently.

Effective Strategies for Addressing Negative Thought Patterns:

Mindfulness and Self-Awareness:

Cultivate mindfulness to observe negative thoughts without judgment. Develop self-awareness to recognize when negative thought patterns emerge.

Cognitive Restructuring:

Challenge and reframe negative thoughts by replacing them with positive, affirming statements. Focus on building a constructive internal dialogue.

Positive Affirmations:

Incorporate positive affirmations into daily routines to counteract negative self-talk. Repeat affirmations that reinforce self-worth and assertiveness.

Gratitude Practice:

Develop a gratitude journal to shift focus from negativity to positive aspects in life. Regularly reflect on achievements and positive experiences.

Professional Support:

Seek guidance from therapists, counselors, or life coaches to address deep-seated negative thought patterns. Professional support can provide tailored strategies for overcoming these challenges.

Behavioral Experiments:

Conduct small, controlled experiments to test negative assumptions. Gradually expose oneself to assertive behaviors, challenging and disproving negative predictions.

Visualization Techniques:

Use visualization to imagine successful, assertive interactions. Create mental scenarios where negative thought patterns are replaced with positive outcomes.

Affirmative Action:

Take small assertive actions regularly to build confidence. Each successful assertive encounter serves as evidence against negative thought patterns.

By actively addressing negative thought patterns, individuals can reshape their mindset and lay the foundation for assertive living. Through consistent practice, self-reflection, and positive reinforcement, one can break free from the constraints of negativity and embrace a more confident, assertive approach to communication and life.

Developing Assertiveness Skills

Assertiveness, a crucial interpersonal skill, can be cultivated and refined with intentional effort and practice. Developing assertiveness skills involves a combination of self-awareness, effective communication techniques, and the courage to express oneself authentically. Let's explore a comprehensive guide to empower individuals on their journey to mastering assertiveness:

1. Self-Reflection:

Understand Your Communication Style:

Reflect on past interactions to identify patterns of behavior. Recognize moments when you leaned towards passivity, aggressiveness, or assertiveness. This self-awareness forms the foundation for improvement.

Identify Personal Boundaries:

Define your boundaries by considering your values, priorities, and comfort levels. Understanding your boundaries is crucial for assertive communication.

2. Learn Effective Communication Techniques:

Use "I" Statements:

Instead of placing blame, express your feelings and needs using "I" statements. For example, say, "I feel overwhelmed with the workload, and I need assistance" rather than "You always assign too much work."

Active Listening:

Practice active listening by fully engaging in conversations. Demonstrate that you value others' perspectives by paraphrasing, summarizing, and asking clarifying questions.

Non-Verbal Communication:

Be mindful of your body language, tone of voice, and facial expressions. Maintain eye contact, use a calm tone, and ensure your non-verbal cues align with your assertive message.

3. Set and Communicate Boundaries:

Clearly Define Boundaries:

Clearly articulate your limits and expectations in various situations, whether at work, in relationships, or within personal commitments.

Practice Saying "No":

Learn to say "no" respectfully and assertively when necessary. Understand that setting boundaries is a healthy and necessary part of self-care.

4. Build Self-Esteem and Confidence:

Acknowledge Achievements:

Celebrate your successes, both big and small. Acknowledging your accomplishments boosts self-esteem and reinforces a positive self-image.

Positive Affirmations:

Incorporate positive affirmations into your daily routine. Remind yourself of your worth, capabilities, and the validity of your thoughts and feelings.

5. Assertiveness Training Programs:

Enroll in Workshops or Courses:

Participate in assertiveness training programs offered by professional organizations, community centers, or online platforms. These programs provide practical tools and guidance for developing assertiveness skills.

6. Gradual Exposure:

Start with Low-Stakes Situations:

Begin by practicing assertiveness in less challenging situations. As you gain confidence, gradually tackle more complex scenarios, such as addressing conflicts or making requests.

Feedback and Reflection:

Seek feedback from trusted individuals after assertive interactions. Reflect on what went well and areas for improvement, adjusting your approach as needed.

7. Role-Playing:

Simulate Scenarios:

Engage in role-playing exercises with a friend, family member, or mentor. Simulating real-life scenarios allows you to practice assertiveness in a supportive environment.

Explore Different Perspectives:

Switch roles during role-playing to gain insight into others' perspectives. Understanding the dynamics from both sides enhances your ability to communicate assertively.

8. Seek Mentorship and Support:

Identify Assertive Role Models:

Seek mentorship from individuals who exhibit assertiveness. Observe their communication styles, seek advice, and learn from their experiences.

Share Goals with a Trusted Support System:

Communicate your assertiveness development goals with friends, family, or mentors. Having a support system provides encouragement and constructive feedback.

9. Apply Assertiveness in Real-Life Situations:

Consistent Practice:

Regularly apply assertiveness skills in various aspects of your life. Consistent practice enhances your ability to communicate assertively in diverse situations.

Learn from Experiences:

Analyze your assertive interactions. Identify successful strategies and areas for improvement. Learning from each experience contributes to continuous growth.

Developing assertiveness skills is an ongoing process that requires dedication and a willingness to step outside your comfort zone. By combining self-reflection, effective communication techniques, and practical exercises, individuals can cultivate assertiveness, leading to more authentic, empowered, and fulfilling communication in both personal and professional spheres.

Assertiveness at Work

In workplace, assertiveness emerges as a potent tool, enabling individuals to navigate challenges, foster collaboration, and contribute meaningfully to their professional environments. Let's explore the essence of assertiveness at work through real-life examples and engaging stories.

1. Clear Communication:

Assertiveness promotes clear and transparent communication, allowing individuals to express their thoughts, ideas, and concerns openly.

Example: Sarah's Team Meeting

Sarah, a team leader, exemplifies assertiveness in team meetings. By fostering an environment where team members feel encouraged to voice their opinions, Sarah not only enhances collaboration but also uncovers innovative solutions.

2. Effective Collaboration:

Assertive communication encourages collaboration by creating a platform for individuals to share expertise and perspectives.

Story: Stuart and Cross-Functional Collaboration

Stuart, a project manager, faces a challenge requiring collaboration across departments. Through assertive communication, he facilitates open discussions, ensuring each team's contributions are acknowledged. The collaborative effort not only resolves the issue but also strengthens interdepartmental relationships.

3. Conflict Resolution:

Assertiveness is instrumental in addressing conflicts constructively, fostering resolutions that benefit all parties involved.

Example: Rekha and Interpersonal Conflict

Rekha, a team member, faces a conflict with a colleague. Rather than avoiding the issue, she employs assertive communication to express her concerns. This approach not only resolves the conflict but also contributes to a more harmonious work environment.

4. Setting Professional Boundaries:

Assertiveness empowers individuals to set and communicate professional boundaries, ensuring a healthy work-life balance.

Story: Thomas and Overtime Boundaries

Thomas, a dedicated employee, establishes assertive boundaries regarding overtime work. By communicating these boundaries clearly, he maintains his well-being and, in turn, enhances his productivity during regular work hours.

5. Assertive Leadership:

Essence: Assertive leaders inspire confidence, guide teams effectively, and contribute to a positive work culture.

Example: Tony's Leadership Style

Tony, a team leader, employs assertive leadership. By fostering open communication, setting clear expectations, and acknowledging team members' contributions, Tony creates a work environment where everyone feels valued and motivated.

6. Professional Development and Recognition:

Assertiveness plays a role in expressing career goals, seeking professional development opportunities, and ensuring recognition for one's contributions.

Story: Chris and Career Advancement

Chris, an ambitious professional, engages in assertive conversations with superiors about career goals and development opportunities. This proactive approach not only leads to personal growth but also positions Chris as an asset within the organization.

7. Handling Feedback Constructively:

Essence: Assertiveness enables individuals to solicit and provide feedback in a constructive manner, fostering continuous improvement.

Example: Ryan's Approach to Feedback

Ryan, a manager, embraces assertiveness when providing feedback to his team. By framing feedback in a positive and solution-oriented manner, he encourages a culture of continuous learning and development.

Assertiveness at work is not just about individual expression; it's a fundamental component of a healthy organizational culture. By embracing assertive communication, individuals contribute to an environment where ideas flow freely, conflicts are addressed constructively, and professional relationships thrive. These real-life examples and stories illustrate the transformative impact of assertiveness on individual and collective success within the workplace.

Assertiveness in Relationships

Assertiveness plays a pivotal role in fostering healthy and authentic relationships, providing a foundation for open communication, mutual respect, and emotional well-being. Let's explore the dynamics of assertiveness in relationships through real-life examples, stories, and insights into both the consequences of lacking assertiveness and potential solutions.

1. Communication and Understanding: Assertiveness in relationships begins with effective communication. Sharing thoughts, feelings, and needs openly contributes to mutual understanding. Consider the story of Emma and Jake, a couple facing challenges in their communication. Emma, lacking assertiveness, would avoid expressing her concerns to Jake, leading to misunderstandings. The consequence was a growing emotional distance. Upon recognizing this pattern, Emma started using 'I' statements to convey her feelings constructively. The solution lay in assertive communication, which not only strengthened their bond but also deepened their understanding of each other.

2. Setting and Respecting Boundaries: Healthy relationships thrive on mutual respect for personal boundaries. Mark and Sarah, a married couple, faced issues when their individual boundaries were not clearly communicated. Mark, feeling overwhelmed

by work, initially hesitated to express his need for personal space. Sarah, unaware of his feelings, unknowingly violated his boundaries. The consequence was mounting tension and frustration. Through assertive communication, Mark conveyed his need for occasional solitude, allowing Sarah to understand and respect his boundaries. This assertive approach not only alleviated tension but also reinforced their commitment to respecting each other's individual needs.

3. Conflict Resolution and Compromise: Assertiveness is a key asset in navigating conflicts constructively. Jessica and Ryan, close friends, found themselves at odds over a disagreement. Initially, both avoided addressing the issue directly, fearing confrontation. The consequence was a strained friendship. Recognizing the importance of assertiveness, they decided to openly discuss their perspectives, using 'I' statements to express feelings. This assertive communication not only resolved the conflict but also strengthened their friendship. The solution lay in a willingness to compromise and a commitment to maintaining open lines of communication.

4. Consequences of Lack of Assertiveness:

Resentment: Suppressing one's needs or feelings can lead to resentment, creating an emotional barrier in the relationship.

Misunderstandings: Lack of assertiveness may result in misunderstandings, as unexpressed thoughts and emotions can be misinterpreted.

Emotional Distance: Over time, a pattern of non-assertive communication can lead to emotional distance and a sense of disconnect.

5. Solutions through Assertiveness:

Open Communication: Foster an environment of open communication, encouraging both partners to express themselves authentically.

Active Listening: Practice active listening to ensure that both perspectives are heard and understood.

Mutual Respect: Cultivate a culture of mutual respect, valuing each other's needs and boundaries.

Conflict Resolution: Approach conflicts with a solution-oriented mindset, using assertiveness to address issues constructively.

Conclusion: Assertiveness in relationships is a dynamic process of self-expression and mutual understanding. Through real-life examples and stories, we see the transformative power of assertiveness in navigating challenges, fostering deeper connections, and promoting emotional well-being. The consequences of lacking assertiveness underscore the importance of cultivating this skill for the sake of healthy and thriving relationships. As individuals embrace assertiveness, they pave the way for richer, more authentic connections that stand the test of time.

Handling Conflict Assertively

Conflict is an inevitable part of human interaction, but how we handle it can shape the course of relationships and professional environments. Assertive conflict resolution involves addressing disagreements openly, expressing concerns, and seeking mutually beneficial solutions. Let's explore key strategies, real-life examples, and stories that illustrate the art of handling conflict assertively.

Strategies for Assertive Conflict Resolution:

Active Listening:

Active listening is a valuable communication strategy that involves actively paying attention to the perspectives of all parties involved. An example of this strategy in action occurred during a team meeting attended by Ramesh. Sensing tension between two colleagues, Ramesh chose to actively listen to both sides of the conflict. Through this attentive approach, he uncovered underlying misunderstandings. By addressing these misunderstandings and providing clarification, Ramesh effectively diffused the tension and contributed to the resolution of the conflict within the team. This exemplifies how the practice of active listening can be instrumental in fostering understanding and resolving disputes in various interpersonal situations.

Expressing Feelings and Needs:

A helpful strategy in expressing feelings and needs is to use 'I' statements. For instance, a person who felt overlooked in a project, assertively communicated his need for recognition. This approach sparked a collaborative discussion among the team members about acknowledging individual contributions. Using 'I' statements allows individuals to share their emotions and requirements in a clear and assertive manner, fostering open communication and understanding in various situations.

Seeking Solutions:

In the pursuit of solutions, the strategy involves working together to find answers that satisfy everyone's concerns. For instance, in a business partnership where conflicting ideas on strategy emerged, assertive communication played a key role. The partners engaged in collaborative discussions, ultimately reaching a middle ground that incorporated elements from both perspectives.

Maintaining Calmness:

Maintaining calmness is crucial in constructive communication. The strategy involves keeping emotions in check to facilitate a positive dialogue. For instance, Maya, faced with a heated discussion at work, took a moment to compose herself. This pause enabled her to address the issue more rationally, leading to a more assertive and productive conversation.

Setting Boundaries:

Setting boundaries is about clearly stating and reinforcing your personal limits, especially during conflicts. For instance, Project manager made it clear that he needed a respectful work environment. He set boundaries against the use of derogatory language, creating a more positive and collaborative atmosphere.

Assertive conflict resolution is not about eliminating conflict but transforming it into an opportunity for growth and understanding. By actively listening, expressing feelings and needs, seeking solutions, maintaining calmness, and setting boundaries, individuals can navigate conflicts assertively, turning potential challenges into stepping stones for positive change.

Improve Assertiveness through Self-Reflection

Self-reflection is a powerful tool for enhancing assertiveness, as it allows individuals to gain deeper insights into their thoughts, emotions, and communication patterns. By engaging in self-reflection, individuals can identify areas for growth, recognize barriers to assertiveness, and develop strategies for more effective communication. Here are methods to improve assertiveness through self-reflection:

Journaling:

Journaling is a valuable practice for personal growth. By regularly jotting down your experiences, interactions, and emotions, you can gain insights into your communication patterns. Reflect on situations where you felt assertive, passive, or aggressive, and note down your feelings during those moments. The purpose of this journaling process is to bring clarity to recurring communication patterns and identify the emotions tied to assertiveness. It serves as a tool for self-reflection, helping you pinpoint areas for improvement and fostering a better understanding of your communication style.

Mindfulness Practices:

Mindfulness practices can be beneficial for enhancing assertiveness. One approach is to incorporate mindfulness meditation or deep-breathing exercises into your daily routine. During assertive, passive, or aggressive moments, pay close attention to your thoughts and feelings. The purpose of these mindfulness practices is to boost self-awareness, allowing you to recognize and understand your reactions and emotions in the moment. By cultivating a calmer mindset through mindfulness, you create space for more intentional and assertive responses in various situations.

Behavioral Analysis:

Behavioral analysis involves a simple yet effective process. Begin by recalling recent situations where assertiveness was needed. Take a close look at both what you said (verbal cues) and how you said it, along with your body language (non-verbal cues). Evaluate the outcomes of these interactions. The purpose is twofold: firstly, to gain insights into how your behavior plays a role in assertiveness, and secondly, to pinpoint areas for improvement in your communication style and overall effectiveness. This introspective process serves as a valuable tool for personal and professional development, helping you refine your approach to assertiveness.

Self-Assessment Tools:

Self-assessment tools are valuable resources for gauging your assertiveness levels. The process involves utilizing assertiveness self-assessment tools or quizzes that can be found online. After completing these assessments, take time to reflect on the results and any feedback provided. The purpose of using these tools is to gain an external perspective on your assertiveness, helping you pinpoint specific areas that might need attention or further development. It's a proactive step in understanding your communication style and identifying areas for personal growth in terms of assertiveness.

Goal Setting:

In the process of goal setting for assertiveness improvement, it's essential to establish specific, measurable, and achievable objectives. Breaking down larger goals into smaller, manageable steps ensures a more systematic approach. The purpose of this goal-setting exercise is to create a clear roadmap for enhancing assertiveness. By setting measurable targets, individuals can track their progress over time. Additionally, breaking down goals into smaller steps makes the journey more manageable and achievable. Celebrating achievements along the way not only acknowledges the effort put in but also serves as motivation for continued progress in the journey toward improved assertiveness.

Role-Playing Scenarios:

Role-playing scenarios provide a practical way to enhance assertive communication skills. In this process, individuals engage in exercises where they practice responding assertively to challenging situations. By playing out scenarios that commonly test assertiveness, participants have the opportunity to develop and refine their assertive communication techniques in a controlled and supportive environment. The purpose of these exercises is to build confidence in expressing oneself assertively across various situations, ultimately transferring these skills to real-life interactions.

Feedback Seeking:

In the process of seeking feedback, start by reaching out to trusted friends, family, or colleagues to gather insights about your communication style. Ask for specific examples and thoughts on your assertiveness. The purpose is to gain external perspectives, allowing you to see how others perceive your assertiveness. The feedback you receive can be constructive, providing valuable guidance for your self-reflection and efforts to improve. By actively seeking input from those around you, you open the door to a clearer understanding of your communication strengths and areas where adjustments can be beneficial.

Visualization Techniques:

Visualization techniques involve a specific process aimed at enhancing assertiveness. The first step is to visualize scenarios in which assertiveness is necessary. Picture yourself clearly expressing your thoughts, needs, and boundaries in these situations. The purpose of this visualization process is to train your mind to respond assertively when faced with similar real-life situations. By creating a mental image of yourself confidently and assertively communicating, you build a positive framework for assertive communication, reinforcing the desired behavior in your mind. This technique leverages the power of visualization to better prepare for assertive interactions in various aspects of life.

Affirmations:

Affirmations play a crucial role in the process of enhancing assertiveness. The first step is to create positive statements or affirmations specifically focused on assertiveness. These affirmations should be repeated regularly, especially before facing challenging situations. The purpose behind this practice is to change any negative self-talk or beliefs one may have about assertiveness. By consistently repeating positive affirmations, individuals aim to cultivate a positive mindset that encourages and supports assertive communication in various aspects of life.

Continuous Evaluation:

Continuous evaluation is a vital aspect of developing assertiveness. The process involves regularly checking how you're doing in terms of being assertive. Take time to think about what's working well and where you face challenges. The purpose of this ongoing assessment is to make sure you keep growing and getting better. By reflecting on your experiences and considering feedback, you can adjust your strategies to align with your evolving self-awareness, contributing to a continuous journey of improvement and development in assertiveness.

By using these self-reflection methods, people can start a journey to become more assertive. This self-thinking not only makes communication better but also helps personal growth, making interactions with others more real and strong.

Improve Assertiveness through Positive Habits

Improving assertiveness is not just about acquiring new skills; it's about surrounding positive habits into your daily life. These habits can gradually transform your communication style, fostering confidence and authenticity. Let's explore methods to enhance assertiveness through positive habits:

Set Clear Intentions:

Setting clear intentions is a helpful habit when it comes to being assertive. Before you start talking with someone, take a moment to decide on your goals for the conversation. This mental roadmap will guide you in expressing yourself in an assertive way. It keeps you focused on communicating constructively and aiming for positive outcomes.

Positive Affirmations:

Positive affirmations can be a powerful tool in fostering assertiveness. By making it a habit to include positive affirmations about assertiveness in your daily routine, you reinforce a positive self-image. This practice serves as a counterbalance to self-doubt, instilling confidence in your communication abilities. Consistently incorporating these affirmations can contribute to a more assertive mindset, positively influencing how you perceive yourself and interact with others in various situations.

Active Listening:

Active listening is a valuable habit that should be practiced in all interactions. The essence of this habit lies in ensuring a thorough understanding of others before expressing your own thoughts. The benefits of active listening are manifold. It not only helps in building rapport with others but also serves as a demonstration of respect. Moreover, active listening lays the groundwork for assertive and effective two-way communication, creating an environment where both parties feel heard and valued.

Body Language Awareness:

Being aware of your body language is crucial for effective communication. Make it a habit to pay attention to how you carry yourself, ensuring that it aligns with assertive communication. This includes maintaining eye contact, having an upright posture, and similar aspects. The benefits of this habit are significant – it enhances the consistency between what you say and how you express it non-verbally. This congruence projects confidence and conviction in your communication, making your message more impactful and authentic.

Constructive Self-Talk:

Engaging in constructive self-talk involves replacing negative inner dialogue with empowering and positive statements. By forming a habit of using language that uplifts and encourages, individuals can transform their mindset, cultivating a more optimistic and assertive approach when faced with communication challenges. This practice not only influences one's internal perspective but also contributes to more effective and confident communication with others, creating a positive ripple effect in personal and professional interactions.

Seek Feedback:

Develop the habit of actively seeking feedback on your assertiveness by reaching out to trusted friends, colleagues, or mentors. This practice comes with numerous benefits, such as gaining valuable insights into your communication style, identifying any blind spots you might have, and creating opportunities for ongoing improvement. By welcoming feedback from those you trust, you enhance your ability to navigate various situations assertively and continually refine your communication skills.

Mindful Communication:

Engaging in mindful communication involves cultivating the habit of practicing mindfulness during conversations. This means staying fully present and focused on the current interaction. The benefits of this practice are numerous. It helps reduce anxiety, allowing individuals to respond thoughtfully rather than react impulsively. Additionally, mindful communication enhances overall effectiveness, fostering a deeper and more meaningful exchange of ideas and information. By being fully present in the moment, individuals can contribute to more positive and constructive interactions, creating a foundation for improved communication.

Embrace Positivity:

Embracing positivity is a key aspect of developing assertiveness. One habit that contributes to this is surrounding yourself with positive influences and opting for environments that encourage assertive communication. Doing so has its benefits—it nurtures a positive mindset, making it more natural for you to express yourself assertively in different situations. By creating a positive and supportive backdrop, you enhance your ability to communicate confidently and effectively.

Celebrate Successes:

Taking the time to celebrate successes is an important habit when it comes to assertiveness. Make it a routine to acknowledge and celebrate moments where you confidently expressed yourself, regardless of how things turned out. Doing this has several benefits—it reinforces positive behavior, gives your confidence a boost, and encourages you to keep approaching communication with assertiveness in a proactive way. Recognizing and celebrating these moments helps create a positive cycle of growth and self-assurance.

Continuous Learning:

Committing to continuous learning is a valuable habit in the journey of personal and professional development. This involves ongoing exploration of assertiveness, communication styles, and related subjects. By making this commitment, you expand your knowledge base, discover new strategies, and reinforce the significance of assertiveness in fostering both personal and professional growth. Embracing a mindset of continuous learning ensures that you stay informed, adaptable, and consistently enhance your skills in navigating various aspects of life.

Visualization Techniques:

Incorporating visualization techniques into your routine can be a valuable habit, especially when it comes to practicing assertive communication. By mentally rehearsing scenarios where you need to assert yourself, you prepare your mind for real-life situations. This mental preparation helps to reduce anxiety and increases the likelihood that you will respond assertively when faced with similar circumstances. Visualization becomes a tool to enhance your confidence and effectiveness in assertive communication.

Gratitude Practice:

Consider incorporating a gratitude practice into your daily routine as a habit to cultivate a positive outlook. Engaging in regular expressions of gratitude can help develop a mindset of abundance, thereby reducing fear and anxiety associated with assertive communication. This simple habit can contribute significantly to creating a more positive and confident approach in your interactions with others.

By integrating these positive habits into your daily life, you create a supportive foundation for improving assertiveness. Over time, these habits become ingrained, transforming the way you communicate and paving the way for more authentic, confident, and assertive interactions.

Improve Assertiveness by Seeking Feedback and Adjusting

The journey towards mastering assertiveness is dynamic, requiring continuous self-reflection and refinement. Seeking feedback from trusted sources and being open to adjustments is a crucial aspect of this ongoing process. Let's explore effective methods for improving assertiveness through feedback and adjustment.

1. Create a Feedback Loop:

Establishing a feedback loop is a crucial step in improving assertiveness. Actively seek constructive feedback from colleagues, friends, or mentors about your assertiveness. Encourage them to provide specific observations on your communication style, how you set boundaries, and handle conflicts. Additionally, set up regular check-ins with key individuals to discuss your progress in developing assertiveness. These check-ins serve as valuable opportunities to receive timely feedback and identify specific areas for improvement. The feedback loop ensures ongoing guidance and allows you to make necessary adjustments to enhance your assertiveness continuously.

2. Reflect on Feedback:

When reflecting on feedback, it's important to engage in objective self-reflection. This means taking a step back and looking at the feedback received without letting personal feelings get in the way. The goal is to separate emotions from constructive observations. Identify any recurring themes or patterns in the feedback, as these can highlight specific areas for improvement. Additionally, consider multiple perspectives by gathering feedback from various sources. Doing so provides a holistic understanding of your assertiveness, as different viewpoints offer valuable insights into various aspects of your communication. Embracing these perspectives contributes to a well-rounded assessment of your communication style.

3. Identify Specific Areas for Improvement:

In the pursuit of improving assertiveness, it's essential to pinpoint specific areas that need enhancement. This involves prioritizing certain aspects of assertiveness, guided by feedback. Key areas for improvement may include enhancing clarity in communication, refining boundary-setting skills, or improving the ability to handle challenging conversations. By focusing on these targeted areas, individuals can direct their efforts toward meaningful growth in assertiveness.

Set Measurable Goals:

Setting measurable goals is a crucial step in the improvement process. It involves defining clear and measurable objectives for enhancement in each identified area. To make the goals more manageable and track progress effectively, it's essential to break down broader objectives into smaller, achievable steps. This approach not only provides a clear roadmap for improvement but also allows for regular assessment and celebration of smaller milestones along the way.

4. Seek Guidance and Training:

To enhance assertiveness, it's beneficial to seek guidance and training. Mentorship is a valuable avenue, where you can learn from individuals who excel in assertiveness. By understanding their experiences and strategies, you can apply relevant techniques to your own development. Additionally, enrolling in assertiveness training programs or workshops provides additional tools and insights. These programs often include role-playing exercises, allowing you to practice assertive communication in a controlled environment. Both seeking mentorship and participating in training programs contribute to a comprehensive approach in improving assertiveness skills.

5. Implement Adjustments:

When implementing adjustments to your communication style, it's beneficial to introduce them gradually. This approach allows for a smooth integration, giving you time to adapt. As you make these changes, carefully monitor their impact and be flexible in refining them based on real-world experiences. This gradual and adaptive process ensures that the adjustments align more effectively with your overall communication goals.

Feedback-Informed Action:

Feedback-Informed Action involves using feedback as a guide for taking specific actions to improve. It's about regularly checking how well the changes you make are working by seeking feedback. This ongoing cycle of getting input and making adjustments based on that feedback is a powerful way to continuously improve and make sure your actions are effective.

6. Assess Impact on Relationships:

As you make adjustments to your assertiveness, it's crucial to assess how these changes impact your relationships. Pay close attention to the dynamics within your relationships, observing whether there's an improvement in communication, mutual understanding, and respect. Foster open communication with the individuals affected by your assertiveness adjustments. Encourage them to share their perspectives and provide feedback on the changes they notice. This ongoing assessment and open dialogue contribute to creating healthier and more effective interpersonal connections.

7. Celebrate Progress:

Celebrating progress on the journey to improved assertiveness is essential. Take a moment to acknowledge and celebrate the milestones you've reached. Recognize the effort you've put into seeking feedback, making adjustments, and consistently working towards positive change. Positive reinforcement is crucial, so be sure to appreciate and reward yourself for the progress you've made. Use these achievements as motivation to continue refining and enhancing your assertiveness. It's a way to recognize your hard work and keep yourself motivated on the path to effective communication and personal growth.

By incorporating these methods into your assertiveness development journey, you create a proactive and feedback-driven approach. Seeking feedback, reflecting on it, and making intentional adjustments contribute to continuous improvement, fostering a communication style that is both authentic and effective.

Conclusion

Assertiveness reveals a variety of skills that go beyond just how we talk to others. It's not only about communication but also about setting boundaries and handling conflicts in a positive way. Being assertive is like having a strong tool that helps build good relationships, boosts self-confidence, and leads to success in both personal and professional parts of life.

It is important to know the differences between it, being too passive, or too aggressive when communicating. Finding the right balance between expressing yourself honestly and respecting others is a key principle as you learn to be more assertive.

Creating boundaries is a crucial part of being assertive. It gives individuals the power to clearly state and communicate their personal limits. When boundaries are communicated strategically, it sets up a structure for positive relationships, avoiding unnecessary stress and fostering an environment where everyone respects each other.

The art of saying 'no' constructively emerges as a key element, allowing individuals to decline requests assertively and honestly. Mastery of this skill is instrumental in avoiding over commitment, maintaining personal well-being, and fostering transparent communication within relationships.

'I' statements, as a communication technique, further elevate assertiveness by providing a framework for expressing feelings, thoughts, and needs without assigning blame. This method not only reduces defensiveness in others but also fosters open and empathetic dialogue, creating an atmosphere conducive to authentic communication.

The significance of assertiveness in professional advancement becomes evident through its role in effective negotiation, leadership development, and overall career success. Real-life examples and stories illustrate how assertive communication empowers individuals to navigate challenges, inspire confidence, and contribute meaningfully to their organizations.

Overcoming barriers to assertiveness involves addressing common challenges such as fear of rejection, conflict avoidance, and low self-esteem. Strategies for overcoming these barriers include self-reflection, seeking feedback, and gradual exposure, empowering individuals to navigate assertiveness with resilience and adaptability.

To keep getting better at being assertive, you need to do a few things over and over. First, ask for feedback, then make changes based on that feedback, and finally, celebrate the improvements you make. This process, along with thinking about how you communicate and making intentional adjustments, helps you talk in a way that's real and fits the different situations in your personal and professional life.

In the broader context of personal and professional development, assertiveness acts as a connecting thread, interlinking effective communication, boundary-setting, and the ability to face challenges with confidence. Mastering assertiveness isn't a static goal; it's an ongoing journey marked by self-discovery, resilience, and a dedication to continual improvement. As individuals embark on this transformative journey, assertiveness evolves beyond being merely a skill, transforming into a guiding principle for living empowered and authentic lives.

Recap of Key Concepts

Assertiveness, a dynamic blend of clear communication, boundary-setting, and conflict resolution, empowers individuals to express themselves authentically while fostering respectful relationships. Let's revisit the fundamental concepts that contribute to the improvement of assertiveness:

Understanding Assertiveness:

Assertiveness is the delicate balance between expressing oneself authentically and respecting the rights and boundaries of others.

It transcends passive or aggressive communication styles, promoting a healthy and assertive approach to interpersonal interactions.

Setting Boundaries:

Setting boundaries involves defining and communicating personal limits to ensure that needs, emotions, and values are respected.

Clarity and consistency in articulating boundaries create a framework for healthy relationships and self-respect.

Saying 'No' Constructively:

Saying 'no' constructively is crucial for avoiding over commitment, maintaining personal well-being, and fostering honesty in relationships.

Offering alternatives, using positive language, and practicing assertive declines are key components of saying 'no' constructively.

Using 'I' Statements:

'I' statements are a communication technique that expresses feelings, thoughts, and needs without assigning blame.

These statements foster open and non-confrontational dialogue, reducing defensiveness in others and promoting empathetic communication.

Professional Advancement:

Assertiveness plays a pivotal role in professional advancement, contributing to effective negotiation, leadership development, and overall career success.

Real-life examples and stories illustrate how assertive communication empowers individuals to navigate challenges and inspire confidence in the workplace.

Overcoming Barriers:

Common barriers to assertiveness include fear of rejection, conflict avoidance, and low self-esteem.

Strategies for overcoming these barriers involve self-reflection, seeking feedback, and gradual exposure, promoting resilience and adaptability.

Seeking Feedback and Adjusting:

Establishing a feedback loop involves soliciting constructive feedback, reflecting on received insights, and identifying specific areas for improvement.

Adjustments are implemented gradually, guided by feedback and real-world experiences, fostering a proactive and feedback-driven approach to assertiveness.

Continuous Improvement:

The journey towards assertiveness is dynamic, marked by continuous self-reflection, openness to feedback, and intentional adjustments.

Celebrating progress and acknowledging achievements serve as positive reinforcement, motivating individuals to persist in their commitment to improving assertiveness.

Therefore, the mastery of assertiveness is a transformative journey that involves understanding its nuances, applying key techniques, and embracing a mindset of continuous improvement. As individuals revisit and reinforce these key concepts, they lay the foundation for a communication style that is both authentic and effective, fostering empowered and fulfilling interactions in both personal and professional spheres.

Annexure: 1

Well done on finishing the book "How to Master Assertiveness." Now, take a moment to consider how assertive you feel. Use the questions below to understand how comfortable you are expressing yourself:

1. In group settings, how likely are you to express your opinions?

    - A) Very likely
    - B) Somewhat likely
    - C) Neutral
    - D) Somewhat unlikely
    - E) Very unlikely

2. When faced with a disagreement, how often do you stand firm on your viewpoint?

    - A) Always
    - B) Often
    - C) Sometimes
    - D) Rarely
    - E) Never

3. How comfortable are you with saying "no" to requests, even if it inconveniences you?

- A) Very comfortable
- B) Comfortable
- C) Neutral
- D) Uncomfortable
- E) Very uncomfortable

4. When initiating conversations with new people, how confident are you?

- A) Very confident
- B) Confident
- C) Neutral
- D) Not very confident
- E) Not confident at all

5. In situations of conflict, how likely are you to address the issue directly?

- A) Always
- B) Often
- C) Sometimes
- D) Rarely
- E) Never

6. How comfortable are you with delegating tasks to others?

- A) Very comfortable
- B) Comfortable
- C) Neutral
- D) Uncomfortable
- E) Very uncomfortable

7. When receiving criticism, how do you typically respond?

- A) Openly and constructively
- B) Defensively but later reflect
- C) Neutral
- D) Feel upset but don't show it
- E) Get defensive and confrontational

8. How often do you openly communicate your needs and desires in personal relationships?

- A) Always
- B) Often
- C) Sometimes
- D) Rarely
- E) Never

9. How comfortable are you with expressing your emotions, both positive and negative?

- A) Very comfortable
- B) Comfortable
- C) Neutral
- D) Uncomfortable
- E) Very uncomfortable

10. In group decision-making, how actively do you contribute your ideas and opinions?

- A) Very actively
- B) Actively
- C) Neutral
- D) Passively
- E) Very passively

11. How often do you find yourself apologizing unnecessarily?

- A) Rarely or never
- B) Occasionally
- C) Neutral
- D) Often
- E) Very often

12. When receiving compliments, how do you usually respond?

- A) Accept gracefully
- B) Downplay or deflect
- C) Neutral
- D) Feel uncomfortable but say thank you
- E) Reject or deny the compliment

13. How assertive are you in negotiating for what you want in various aspects of your life?

- A) Very assertive
- B) Assertive
- C) Neutral
- D) Somewhat passive
- E) Very passive

14. How comfortable are you with asserting your boundaries in different situations?

- A) Very comfortable
- B) Comfortable
- C) Neutral
- D) Uncomfortable

- E) Very uncomfortable

15. Do you often avoid expressing your true feelings to maintain harmony?

    - A) Rarely or never

    - B) Occasionally

    - C) Neutral

    - D) Often

    - E) Very often

16. How confident are you in expressing disagreement with authority figures?

    - A) Very confident

    - B) Confident

    - C) Neutral

    - D) Not very confident

    - E) Not confident at all

17. How often do you find yourself going along with others' decisions to avoid conflict?

    - A) Rarely or never

    - B) Occasionally

    - C) Neutral

    - D) Often

- E) Very often

18. When making decisions, how much do you consider your own preferences and desires?

    - A) Always

    - B) Often

    - C) Sometimes

    - D) Rarely

    - E) Never

19. How assertive do you feel in communicating your expectations to others?

    - A) Very assertive

    - B) Assertive

    - C) Neutral

    - D) Somewhat passive

    - E) Very passive

20. How often do you find yourself avoiding difficult conversations to maintain peace?

    - A) Rarely or never

    - B) Occasionally

    - C) Neutral

    - D) Often

- E) Very often

Scoring:

- For each "A" answer, assign 5 points
- For each "B" answer, assign 4 points
- For each "C" answer, assign 3 points
- For each "D" answer, assign 2 points
- For each "E" answer, assign 1 point

Calculate the total score to determine assertiveness level.

Grading System for Assertiveness Score:

- **25 - 50 points:** Low Assertiveness

    You may struggle with asserting yourself in various situations. Consider exploring assertiveness techniques to enhance your communication skills.

- **51 - 75 points:** Moderate Assertiveness

    Your assertiveness level is moderate, but there's room for improvement. Focus on strengthening your assertiveness skills for more effective communication.

- **76 - 100 points:** High Assertiveness

    Congratulations! Your assertiveness level is high. You demonstrate confidence in expressing yourself and maintaining healthy boundaries. Continue honing your skills for even more impactful communication.